This

Nature Storybook

belongs to:

For
Bronwyn and Daphne;
Isabel, Sam and Oliver;
Blue and Beau;
and Max – with lots
and lots of love
N. D.

For
Mick, with love
B. G.

First published 2011 by Walker Books Ltd
87 Vauxhall Walk, London SE11 5HJ

This edition published 2013

2 4 6 8 10 9 7 5 3 1

Text © 2011 Nicola Davies
Illustrations © 2011 Brita Granström

The right of Nicola Davies and Brita Granström to
be identified as author and illustrator respectively
of this work has been asserted by them in
accordance with the Copyright, Designs
and Patents Act 1988

This book has been typeset in Ice Age D

Printed in China

British Library Cataloguing in Publication Data:
a catalogue record for this book is available
from the British Library

ISBN 978-1-4063-4401-1

www.walker.co.uk

WALKER BOOKS
AND SUBSIDIARIES
LONDON • BOSTON • SYDNEY • AUCKLAND

Dolphin Baby

NICOLA DAVIES

illustrated by BRITA GRANSTRÖM

Tail first, head last,
Dolphin POPS out
into the blue.

He's creased and crinkled
from being curled inside his
mother. His tail flukes are
floppy from being folded for
so long. He's all brand
new, but straightaway,
he swims up ... up ...

Baby dolphins are born one at
a time, and are called calves.

up...

Pppfffff!

His blowhole opens when it touches air,
and he takes his first breath.

Mum is right beside him and they breathe together in perfect time.

Pppfffff!

Ppppfffff!

Dolphins are mammals like you and me, so although they live all their lives in the sea, they must come to the surface to breathe air.

When Mum swims, Dolphin knows that
he must follow. Swimming and following
are things baby dolphins are
born knowing ...

but suckling
takes a little
practice.

Newborn dolphins suckle two
or three times every hour,
for just a few seconds
each time.

Dolphin dives beneath his mother to find one of her nipples tucked into slits under her belly. It takes him a while to get it right, and then he needs to take another breath or two.

Dolphins communicate
with lots of different
whistles.

Mum and Dolphin rest together.
Dolphin rubs his tummy on Mum's
round head. Mum strokes him
with her flipper. She whistles him
the whistle that is just hers –
her name in dolphin-sound:

Shreeee-eep!

He whistles back – but for now
his whistles make no sense ...
they're baby-talk!

*Every dolphin has one whistle that's its own,
a bit like our human names.*

Others have arrived to take
a look at newborn Dolphin.
They're all around.
Their voices fill the water.
They're curious about
this new member
of their group.

14

But Mum knows that what
new babies need is peace
and quiet. Soon she
swims away, with
Dolphin close
beside her.

Dolphins are very sociable and live in
close groups of around 15, which split up
and re-form all the time.

In just a few weeks, Dolphin's grown so much! His folds and creases are all gone: he's smooth and grey. He doesn't swim beside Mum now, the way newborn babies do, but underneath her tail like **bigger** calves.

Male calves make best friends with one or two other males that they'll know all their lives.

Now he's old enough to make friends.
The youngsters play –
chasing ... carrying ... showing off ...

but then Mum whistles,
and Dolphin knows he must go back.

Playing can't take
all day. Mum
needs to swim off
and hunt for food.
Dolphin stays close,
but sometimes ...

Adult dolphins spend about a third of every day hunting and eating.

she ZOOMS after fish,
too fast for him to follow ...

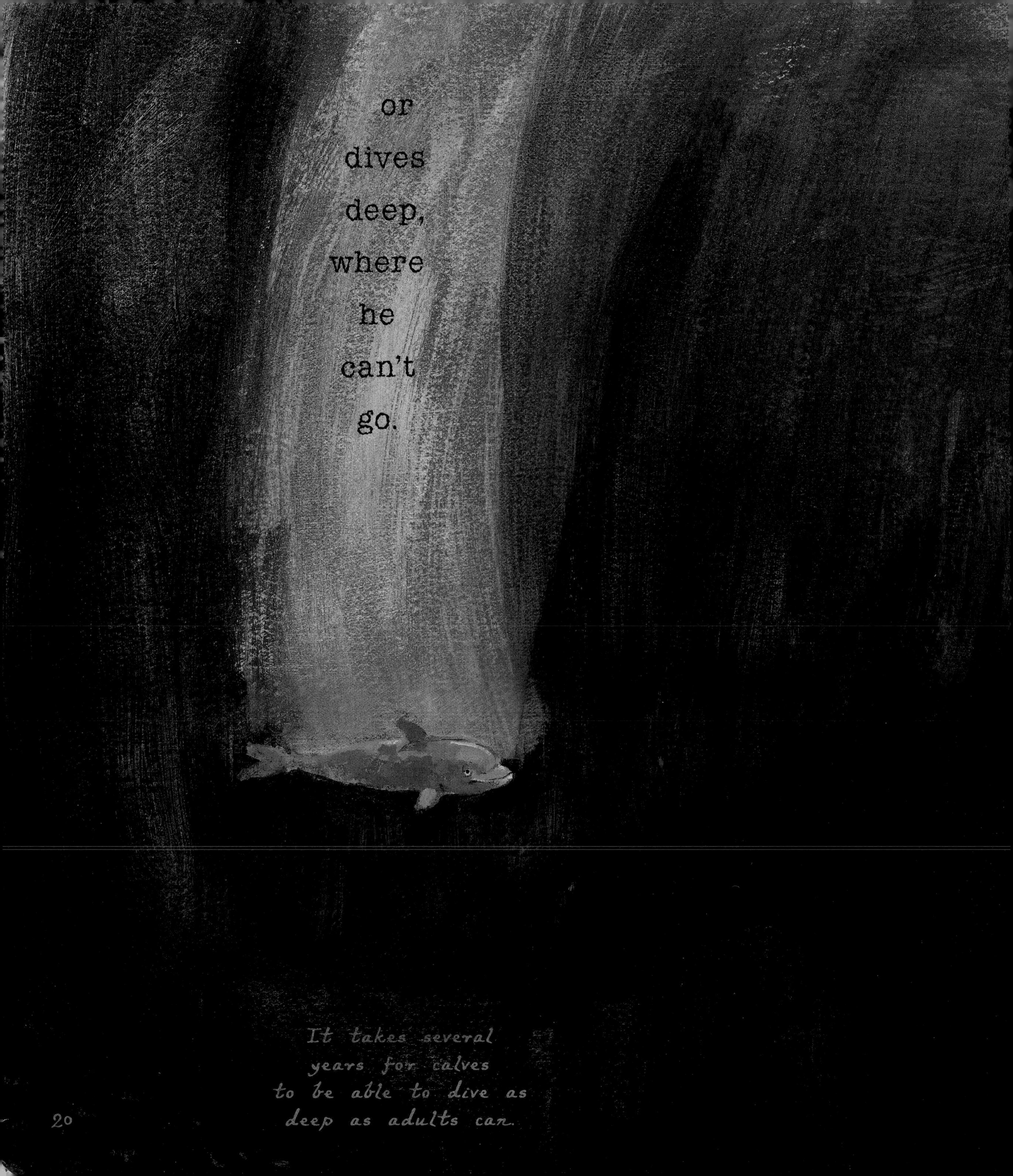

or

dives

deep,

where

he

can't

go.

*It takes several
years for calves
to be able to dive as
deep as adults can.*

Dolphin hears her C L I C K I N G,
using sounds and echoes to find food
where it's too dark or deep for her to see.

He clicks too, and listens to the echoes of his
voice so he can hear Mum's shape and movement
when she's out of sight.

A dolphin's round head is called a melon.
It helps it to make clicks and find
its way around using sound.

21

Mum doesn't stay away for long.
She whistles, *Shreeee-eep!*
when she's coming back. She brings
a fish for Dolphin – still alive.

He C L I C K S at it,
to learn the echo-shape it makes,
so one day he can catch his own.

Then Mum eats it up in two quick bites.
No need to share, as Dolphin is
still fed by her milk.

Dolphins usually hunt for fish alone and
don't share food, even with their calves.

It's SIX months now since Dolphin popped into the blue. He's not a grown-up yet, but he's not a baby any more ...

because today

24

Dolphin's caught his first fish!

Snacking on fish near the surface is just one of many ways dolphins learn to catch their dinner.

And when Mum
whistles her
sound-name,
Shreee-eep!
he doesn't whistle
back in baby-talk,
but answers
with a whistle
that's his very own,
Eeee-SEEP!
This whistle will be
his for all his life.

His name, in Dolphin.

Dolphin calves stay with
their mums for about
four years. They start
to have babies at about
12, and can live for 20
or 30 years in the wild.

TAKING CARE OF DOLPHINS

There are more than 30 different kinds of dolphin in the world, including dusky dolphins, white-sided dolphins, spinner dolphins, spotted dolphins and striped dolphins. The ones in this book are bottlenose dolphins, which are found in almost every ocean except the very coldest ones.

I've been lucky enough to see them in lots of different places, from chilly grey seas to warm tropical ones, and wherever they are, bottlenose dolphins are always ready to play. They jump out of the water, do somersaults and back flips, and bow ride at the front of boats. Watching them is a delight.

Right now, there are still plenty of bottlenose dolphins in the world's oceans, but they are threatened by the risk of being caught in fishing nets; by pollution, and by over-fishing which takes away their food. We need to take better care, so that our seas will stay full of dolphins and dolphin babies for centuries to come.

N. D.

INDEX

Look up the pages to find out about all these dolphin things. Don't forget to look at both kinds of word – this kind and *this kind*.

blowhole ... 8

breathing ... 8–9, 11

calves ... 6, 16–17, 20, 23, 26

clicking ... 21, 23

diving ... 20

echoes ... 21, 23

fish ... 19, 22–23, 25

following ... 10, 19

hunting ... 19, 23

playing ... 17–18, 28

suckling ... 10–11

swimming ... 6, 10, 15–16, 18

tail ... 6, 16

tummy ... 13

whistling ... 12–13, 17, 22, 26

Praise for Nature Storybooks...

"For the child who constantly asks How? Why?
and What For? this series is excellent."
The Sunday Express

"A boon to parents seeking non-fiction picture books to read
with their children. They have excellent texts
and a very high standard of illustration to go with them."
The Daily Telegraph

"As books to engage and delight children, they work superbly.
I would certainly want a set in any primary
classroom I was working in."
Times Educational Supplement

"Here are books that stand out from the crowd,
each one real and individual in its own right and
the whole lot as different from most other series non-fiction
as tasty Lancashire is from processed Cheddar."
Books for Keeps

Find notes for teachers about how to use Nature Storybooks in the classroom at
www.walker.co.uk/downloads

Nature Storybooks support KS 1-2 Science